CHARLES FIRTH'S FRACTURED FAIRY TALES

First published in 2019.

The Chaser's Disclaimer

Managing editor: Charles Firth. This is, amazingly, the sixteenth issue of The Chaser Quarterly, and is published by Chaser Quarterly Pty Ltd (ACN 141758812) of 27/57 Hereford St, Glebe, NSW, 2037. No effort has been made to verify any facts contained within this publication and so no responsibility will be taken for errors or omissions contained herein by Chaser Quarterly Pty Ltd, its officers, employees or their agents. Readers should rely on their own enquiries when making decisions touching on their interests. Apart from satirical articles which discuss public figures for the purposes of humour, any mention of any person, alive or dead, is entirely coincidental. We expect readers to use their own common sense in determining the truth or otherwise of any statement in this publication. They're fucking Fairy Tales, for God's sake. The Chaser Quarterly is available in bookshops across Australia, and is printed by Spotpress, 24-26 Lilian Fowler Pl, Marrickville, NSW, 2204. Subscribe at chasershop.com and stay up to date at chaser.com.au

Cataloguing in Publication details are available from the National Library of Australia

www.trove.nla.gov.au or at least until Morrison scraps its funding

Myers-Briggs personality type:

ISBN 9781760641450

Editor: Veronicah Larkin (Who you should not blame for all the last minute typos we added in)

Chaser editor: Cam Smith

Illustrators: Rania Mahmoud (The Boy Who Wanted a Friend and The One Bad Prince), Glitchfool (Golden Child and the Three Bears), Chiara Corradett (The Handsome Troll and the Professor) and Sabdo "Oketoon" (Mr Archimedes' Bath)

Set in 18 pt Old Standard TT from the "Extremely Unoriginal Fairytale Book Font Pack"

Printed, bound, gagged, and left unconscious on a popular hiking trail by Spotpress

10 9 8 7 6 5 4 3 2 1 Ready or not here we come.

The paper in this book is 100% sourced from re-used soiled toilet paper, to better match the quality of the comedy throughout.

CONTENTS

Introduction	8
The Boy Who Wanted a Friend	13
The Handsome Troll and the Professor	33
Golden Child and the Three Bears	55
Mr Archimedes' Bath	91
The One Bad Prince	107

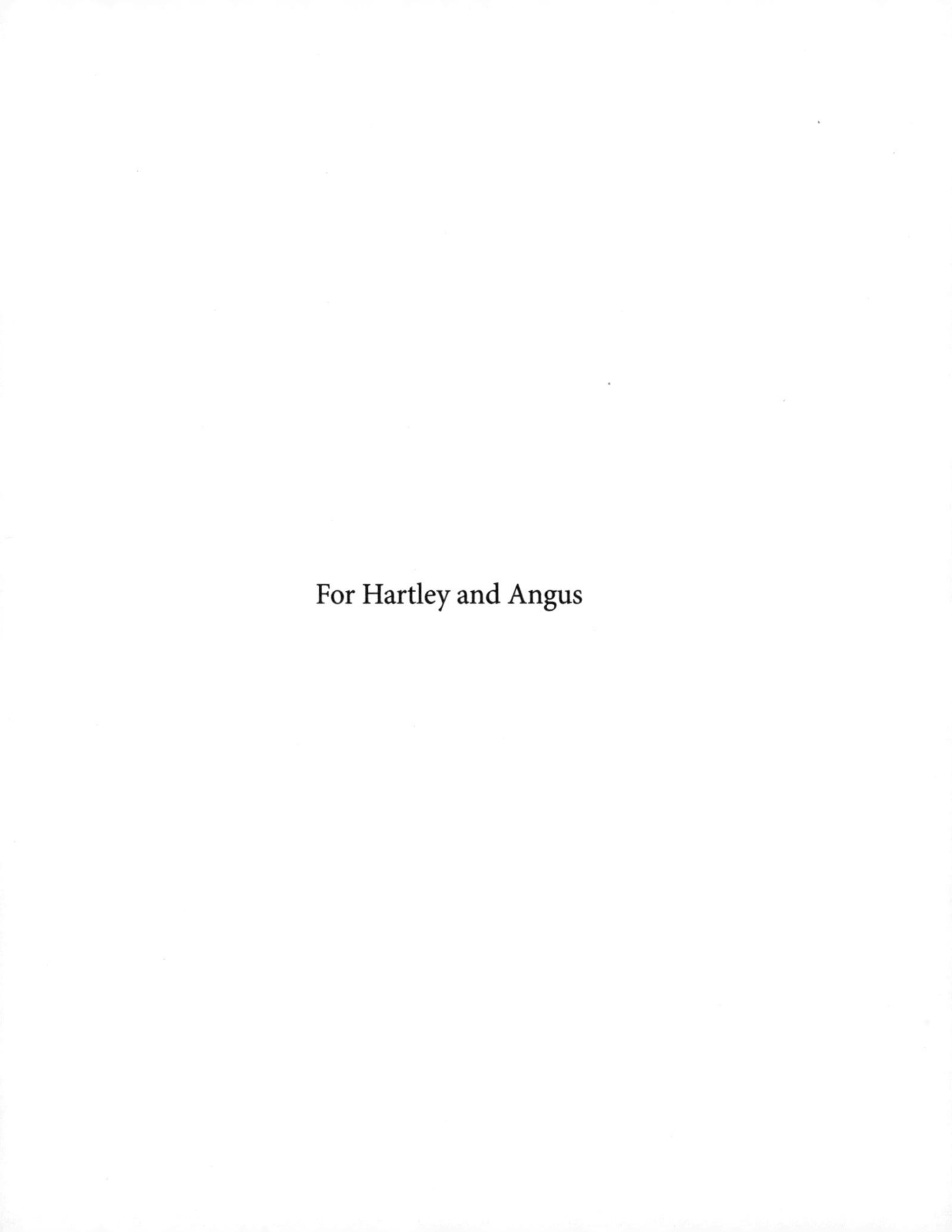

For Hartley and Angus

INTRODUCTION

Once upon a time, a long time ago, the world was ruled by royals and their noble men and women.

Everyone was enslaved by a small number of very rich people, who owned all the land and lived lavish lives, while all the peasants toiled away endlessly at their pitifully boring jobs, paying large portions of their wealth to the rich landowners, while the rich barons paid nothing because they wrote the laws. The peasants' life was so bad even the final season of their favourite television show was lacklustre.

Then one day, the good people of the world banded together and overthrew these wicked royals, and there was much rejoicing.

At last, people would be equal. Rich people would pay their fair share and, best of all, television would be free.

However, at the last minute, just as a global utopia was about to happen, someone suggested that, instead of making everything fair, perhaps they should go back to how things had always been.

Unfortunately, this suggestion was made at the same time that the very final episode of M*A*S*H was on, so nobody paid attention to it, and it became law of the land.

Soon, the air became poison, the seas started to boil, and, worst of all, you now had to subscribe to eight streaming platforms just to keep up with the shows you wanted to watch.

As the world slowly fell to pieces, so too did the fairy tales. The jungle from the *Jungle Book* was logged and became a mini mall.

The world of *Frozen* quickly succumbed to global warming and became a large puddle. Prince Charming got put on the sex offender list for kissing women in their sleep.

Even the *Little Mermaid* ended up as a plate of sashimi after being dragged up as "collateral overcatch" by a fishing trawler.

What's more, instead of children suffering at the hands of evil step-parents, the world's youth simply suffered at the hands of their regular parents, who elected evil governments in exchange for gifts like negative gearing, franking credits, and the promise that they would be able to retire in luxury using the vast sums of money the next generation would be forced to pay for their houses.

So how do we teach modern people the error of their ways? Well, they certainly don't seem to listen to science or reason, that's for sure. Sadly, the truth is boring and depressing.

In the age of the internet, the only things people will listen to is made-up facts. In fact, the more made-up and unbelievable they sound the better!

Did you once read something about how eating like a caveman is good for you? Sounds unlikely, so it must be true.

Think Hillary Clinton is secretly running a sex-ring out of a pizza parlor? Wow, surely nobody would make up something that outlandish, so it must be true. Think vaccines cause autism? Look, actually, we're not going to joke about that one, because its so terrifyingly stupid THAT IT MUST BE TRUE.

And so, to convince you all that yes the world is currently about to burn down in a catastrophe of our own making, in the following pages we will present some parables so unbelievable, so clearly made up, you'll be unable to resist believing them.

Cam Smith
Editor
June, 2019

- Chapter One -

The Boy Who Wanted a Friend

Once upon a time, there was a boy who wanted a friend.

Though he was very smart, the boy didn't know how to make friends.

So he wrote a magic computer program that would make every girl he knew become his friend.

Soon, everyone he knew was his friend, and more besides.

The computer program told him he had more friends than he had ever dreamed possible.

But the boy still did not feel like he had enough friends. So he kept programming his computer to search for more friends.

His computer program searched through all the lands in the world to find the boy more friends. Soon everyone in the world was his friend.

But the boy still did not feel that he had enough friends.

Soon, the king's advisor came to the boy, and told him that the king had a generous gift. "The king will give you lots of gold coins," she said. "More gold coins than anyone has ever had, ever."

“I don’t care much about gold coins,” said the boy. “I just want more friends.”

The king's advisor thought about this for a moment. She knew the king really wanted the boy to accept the king's gift. "If you accept the gold, then perhaps you can buy more friends?" she asked, hopefully.

The boy knew it was not possible to buy friends. But with the gold coins, perhaps the boy could buy his friends presents, and make them like him even more.

And so the boy accepted the gold coins from the king. And in return, the boy told the king's advisor everything he knew about everyone across the world, which didn't seem like a bad deal.

After all, it meant the boy got to spend more time with the king's advisor, whom he quite liked.

The boy wondered whether the king's advisor would be his friend.

But as soon as she had all the information in all of the world, she left.

She didn't even say goodbye to the boy.

The boy felt sad. Even though everyone in the world was his friend, he felt like the loneliest boy in the world.

Then the boy realised. His friends weren't really his friends. They were his enemies.

And he would teach them a lesson.

He programmed his computer. He programmed it all day and all night.

Eventually, he finished.

The boy had programmed his computer to divide everyone in the world into little groups. Now he would make them fight against each other.

And he would sit back and watch on and laugh at them.

The boy didn't need a friend after all.

- Chapter Two -

The Handsome Troll and the Ugly Professor

Once upon a time, in a land far away for tax purposes, a handsome troll discovered a mine full of special gems.

The special gems were very powerful.

The gems allowed people to fly.

They allowed people to make night into day.

They allowed the king to hold big parties at any time of the night or day.

And so the troll got very rich selling the gems.

In fact, the kings and queens of many lands declared the handsome troll to be a prince, as long as he kept selling them his special gems.

Soon the whole world was awash with gems.

Boys wore them in their hair.

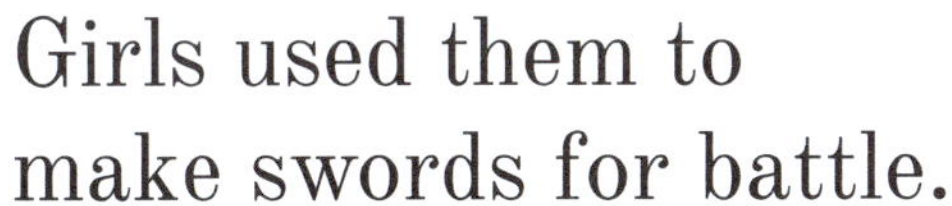

Girls used them to make swords for battle.

Everyone used the gems to make bags with which to carry things.

One day, the troll announced that he had found a tall, tall mountain that was made entirely of gems.

There were so many gems in the tall, tall mountain that everyone could have anything they wanted.

Princesses could have as many racing cars as they liked.

Princes could have as many gems to wear on their smart suits as they wished.

The townsfolk were overjoyed. They held a big party to celebrate.

At the party, an ugly professor stepped forward. He turned off the music, and announced that he had discovered something very bad about the gems.

“Every time anyone uses a special gem,” he said, “The Tree of Life gets sicker.”

Everyone at the party gasped. The Tree of Life was the tree that kept everything on earth alive.

They knew that if the tree died, then everything on earth would die too.

The queen did not know what to do. She asked her three most trusted advisors to come forward.

The first advisor told her that the only solution was to leave the gems in the ground.

"But how can we do this?" asked the queen. "If there are no more gems, then planes will not fly and the lights will not work. Worst of all, this party will have to be cancelled."

The first advisor said "That's not my concern. My only concern is making sure the gems are not used. I'm sure the townsfolk will work something out."

The queen thought about it. "No. Too many people will suffer if we do it your way."

The second advisor stepped forward and told the queen that the gems must stay in the ground, but it was important not to tell anyone in case they got upset.

"People like their planes and their lights and their parties," whispered the second advisor. "Let's just pretend that everyone can have as many gems as they like. Then, when the troll is not looking, we'll take away his spade, and he won't be able to dig any more gems out of the mountain."

The queen thought about this idea. "No," she said at last. "Your way is dishonest and tricky and people will not trust me if we do it your way."

The third advisor stepped forward. The queen was surprised to see that the third advisor was the handsome troll himself.

“Hello Queen!” he said, with a broad smile on his face.

He took off his baseball cap and spoke.

“The ugly professor is a good friend of mine. I believe everything he has to say,” the troll said. “But look at this beautiful sword I have made for you, made of the finest gems. And look at this magnificent brooch. Do you really want a world without these items of beauty?”

Before the queen had a chance to respond, the handsome troll continued, “But above all, look up in the sky!”

The queen and all the townsfolk looked up in the sky, and saw the most amazing fireworks display they had ever seen. They gasped at the sheer beauty and excitement.

The party was a huge success and, by the morning, everyone had forgotten about the ugly professor's warning.

And so the handsome troll dug up his mountain of gems.

And everyone died the following winter.

- Chapter Three -

Golden Child and the Three Bears

Once upon a time, there was Mummy Bear, Daddy Bear and Baby Bear.

Mummy Bear was a doctor who worked at the hospital.

When people had a sore tummy, they would come to her and she would fix them. Each day, she was paid three gold coins.

Daddy Bear was also a doctor.

When people had a sore throat, they would come to him and he would fix them. Each day, he was paid four gold coins.

That night, Mummy Bear got home and cooked the dinner, while Daddy Bear looked at his phone.

Baby Bear said to Mummy Bear, “You always cook the dinner, while Daddy looks at his phone. Why?”

“Because that’s how it works,” replied Mummy Bear.

The next morning, Mummy Bear was folding the laundry, while Daddy Bear sat on the toilet.

Baby Bear said to Mummy Bear, “You always fold the laundry. Why?”

Mummy Bear sighed and replied, “Because that’s how it works.”

But Baby Bear wanted to know more.

“Why is that how it works?” she asked.

“Many years ago, the king decreed that Daddy Bears should sit on the toilet while Mummy Bears folded the washing,” Mummy Bear said to Baby Bear, “and that Daddy Bears should look at their phones, while Mummy Bears cooked the dinner, and that when they go to work, Daddy Bears should get paid more gold coins than Mummy Bears. That’s why.”

Baby Bear was not looking forward to being a Mummy Bear.

Restaurant

The next night, Mummy Bear proclaimed that it was Daddy Bear's turn to cook the dinner for once.

And so Daddy Bear decided that the Bear family would all go out for dinner to a restaurant.

While they were gone, a charming prince walked by the Bear family's house. The charming prince was the son of the king.

He noticed there were no lights on at the Bear family's house.

He knocked on the door. There was no answer.

And so the charming prince opened the door and crept into the house.

He saw the chairs and the tables and the beds of the Bear family.

“These bears are not as rich as me,” the charming prince said to himself. “But these are not poor bears, either.”

“These are middle-class bears,” the prince proclaimed.

The charming prince searched through the house and stole everything he could.

He stole Baby Bear's precious toy.

He stole Daddy Bear's precious phone.

The Second Sex
by Simone de Beauvoir.

He stole Mummy Bear’s precious copy of *The Second Sex* by Simone de Beauvoir.

Just as he was about to leave the Bear family's house, Mummy Bear, Daddy Bear and Baby Bear arrived home.

"What are you doing in our house?" asked Mummy Bear.

"I am stealing all your stuff," said the charming prince.

Shocked, the three bears called the royal guards.

The guards took the charming prince away, to be tried for his crimes.

The next day, the charming prince was brought before the king.

The charming prince bowed his head, waiting for his punishment.

"You will not be punished," declared the king. "Instead, I am promoting you to the position of CEO of King's Bank. From now on, you will be in charge of all finances in all of the kingdom."

A parade was called to celebrate.

Baby Bear turned to Mummy Bear.

"But why was the charming prince not punished?" she asked.

"Because that's how it works," replied Mummy Bear.

- Chapter Four -

Mr Archimedes and his bath

Mr Archimedes enjoyed his baths.

Every night, Mr Archimedes would run a nice hot bath and listen to his favourite podcast about a mean old king who wanted to build a wall.

His bath was the one thing that let Mr Archimedes relax, even though he was in a dead-end job with no hope of achieving any of his life goals.

One day, Mr Archimedes was enjoying his bath, dreaming of a life not lived, when he noticed that the water level in the bath was rising.

It was getting higher and higher.

Mr Archimedes checked the taps.

The water was not flowing and yet the bath water rose higher and higher.

Mr Archimedes checked to see if his dog had climbed into the bath.

His dog was not in the bath and yet the bath water rose higher and higher.

Mr Archimedes checked to see whether there was a leak in the roof that was flowing into the bath.

There was no leak and yet the bath water rose higher and higher.

Then Mr Archimedes noticed that a large block of ice was at the other end of his bath.

As the block of ice melted, the bath water rose higher and higher.

Mr Archimedes looked around. There was a large log fire burning at the other end of the bath too.

All he had to do was douse the fire with some bath water and the ice would stop melting into the bath.

Just as Mr Archimedes was about to put out the fire, a charming prince appeared.

"What are you doing here?" Mr Archimedes asked the prince.

"I am here to offer you this special gold coin," said the prince.

"That doesn't sound too bad," said Mr Archimedes. "What's the catch?"

"There is no catch," said the prince. "As long as you do nothing about the melting ice, I will reward you with this gold coin and many more besides."

Mr Archimedes looked at the ice. And then he looked at the coin.

He thought about all the wonderful things he could buy with the gold coin. If he had a gold coin, he would hold a big party and invite lots of people, who would all want to be his friend.

Mr Archimedes took the coin from the charming Prince, then lay down in the bath, and dreamed of all the things he would buy for his party.

The water level rose higher and higher.

Mr Archimedes did not douse the fire that was melting the ice.

Mr Archimedes would buy lots of chips. He would buy lots of drinks. And everyone would love him.

The water rose over Mr Archimedes' lips.

He did not douse the fire. He thought about the lollies he would buy for his party.

The water rose over Mr Archimedes' nose.

He thought about the decorations that he would buy for his party. They would be bright colours. He loved the colour yellow. That would be the colour of his party.

Eventually, the water rose over Mr Archimedes and he drowned.

But he drowned a rich and happy man.

- Chapter Five -

The One Bad Prince

Once upon a time a beautiful princess from a distant land arrived at the king's palace.

"I have a message," she said, before collapsing on the doorstep.

So exhausted was she by her journey that she lay in bed for 40 days and 40 nights, watching television, and refusing to speak to anyone.

The king's courtiers wondered what her message could be.

"She is very beautiful," said one guardsman. "So when she awakes, we must listen to her."

"Yes," agreed a second guardsman. "Whether you should listen to a princess or not should mainly be determined by how beautiful she is."

But a third guardsman disagreed. "We should listen to her, whether she is beautiful or not."

The courtiers all looked at the third guardsman as if he were an idiot. "No we shouldn't," they shouted at him. He was banished to the dungeon, where he couldn't even watch television.

When the princess finally awoke, she went to the king, and told him that she had a terrible tale to tell.

“Many years ago,” she said, “Prince Harvey visited my castle.”

The king’s courtiers gasped at this news. Prince Harvey was the king’s meanest son. But he was also very powerful. Prince Harvey had the power to decide who could wear a tiara to the Royal Ball.

It was a power that meant every princess in the land had to be nice to the prince, no matter how nastily he behaved.

The princess went on. “After he arrived at my castle, he tried to kiss me, even though I didn’t want to be kissed.”

The courtiers gasped in shock at the news, even though all of them had heard of Prince Harvey doing similar things to other princesses.

"After I refused his kiss, Prince Harvey told me I could never wear a tiara ever again. He said he would cast a spell which meant that people would instantly forget my name the moment I left their sight."

The courtiers gasped in shock, though they had heard of Prince Harvey doing similar things to other princesses.

“This is unacceptable in my kingdom!” declared the king.

The princess said that she had other tales of other princes doing equally terrible things.

"Be quiet!" commanded the king to the princess. "I have heard enough. Prince Harvey shall be punished. But he will be

the only one punished. I don't want to hear about anyone else."

And so the king held a big party to celebrate how good he was for punishing one bad prince.

At the party, the princess walked up to the king.

"You punished a man who had done something wrong. That is a bold thing to do. I have never seen that happen before," the princess told the king.

"Who are you?" replied the king.

"I am the Princess. The one who reported Prince Harvey's evil ways," said the princess.

"I'm sorry, I have no idea who you are," replied the king.

The princess was shocked.

“But you are very beautiful,” said the king, “so perhaps you would like to have my hand in marriage, and be my queen?”

“I’d rather rot in a dungeon,” replied the princess.

“And so it shall be,” said the king.

And so the beautiful princess was thrown into the dungeon and she never watched television again.

THE END

The Official Guide to Election 2019 - $19.95

The Chaser and Shovel Annual 2018 - $24.95

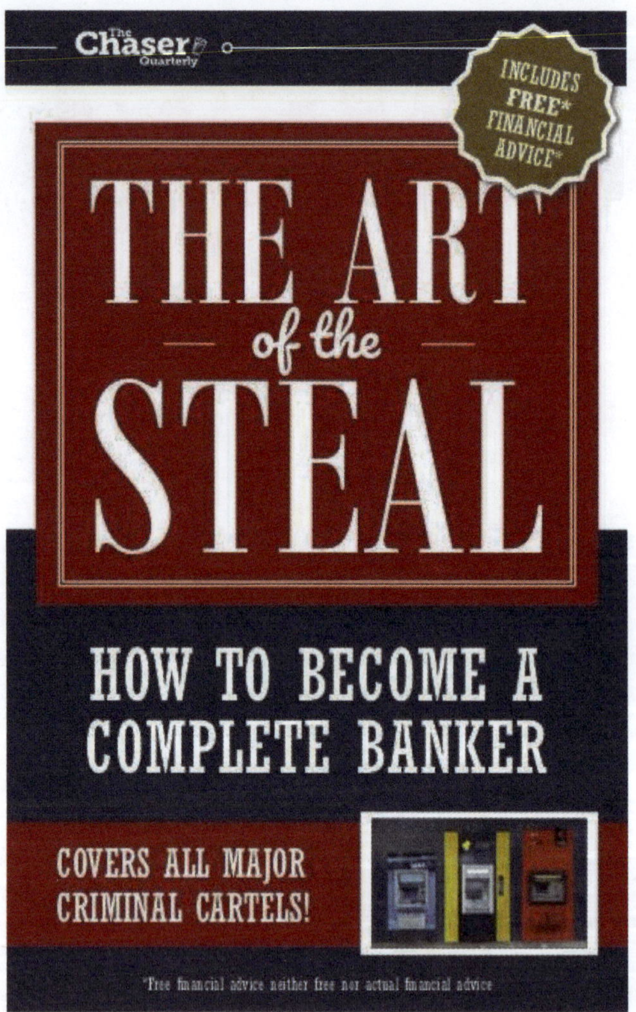

The Art of the Steal - $19.95